D1542005

HIP-HOP
ARTISTS

CARDI B

GROUNDBREAKING RAP **POWERHOUSE**

BY AUDREY DeANGELIS

Essential Library
An Imprint of Abdo Publishing
abdobooks.com

ABDOBOOKS.COM

Published by Abdo Publishing, a division of ABDO, PO Box 398166, Minneapolis, Minnesota 55439. Copyright © 2020 by Abdo Consulting Group, Inc. International copyrights reserved in all countries. No part of this book may be reproduced in any form without written permission from the publisher. Essential Library™ is a trademark and logo of Abdo Publishing.

Printed in the United States of America, North Mankato, Minnesota.
082019
012020

THIS BOOK CONTAINS
RECYCLED MATERIALS

Cover Photo: Featureflash Photo Agency/Shutterstock Images
Interior Photos: Jordan Strauss/Invision/AP Images, 4; Katherine Welles/ Shutterstock Images, 6; Rob Latour/Rex Features, 8–9, 10; Matt Baron/Rex Features, 14; Gregory James Van Raalte/Shutterstock Images, 16–17; Ilya Kuzniatsou/ Shutterstock Images, 22; Tinseltown/Shutterstock Images, 25; Lev Radin/ Shutterstock Images, 26; J. Stone/Shutterstock Images, 28, 56; Rob Kim/Getty Images Entertainment/Getty Images, 32; Mediapunch/Rex Features, 35, 74–75; Alberto E. Tamargo/Sipa/AP Images, 37; Abel Fermin/WWD/Rex Features, 38; Feature Flash Photo Agency/Shutterstock Images, 42–43; Rex Features, 45, 50–51; Broadimage/Rex Features, 48–49, 62–63; Prince Williams/WireImage/Getty Images, 54; Denis Makarenko/Shutterstock Images, 59; Matteo Chinellato/Shutterstock Images, 60; Shutterstock Images, 64–65, 71; Doug Peters/starmaxinc.com/ Newscom, 66; Wenn/AP Images, 72–73; Erin Alexis Randolph/Shutterstock Images, 77; John G Mabanglo/EPA/Rex Features, 81; ImageSpace/Rex Features, 85; AFF-USA/Rex Features, 86; Kevin Mazur/Getty Images Entertainment/Getty Images, 88–89; Suzanne Cordeiro/AFP/Getty Images, 92–93; Scott Dudelson/Coachella/ Getty Images Entertainment/Getty Images, 95; Amy Harris/Invision/AP Images, 97

Editor: Megan Ellis
Series Designer: Laura Graphenteen

LIBRARY OF CONGRESS CONTROL NUMBER: 2019941950
PUBLISHER'S CATALOGING-IN-PUBLICATION DATA

Names: DeAngelis, Audrey, author.
Title: Cardi B: groundbreaking rap powerhouse / by Audrey DeAngelis
Other title: groundbreaking rap powerhouse
Description: Minneapolis, Minnesota : Abdo Publishing, 2020 | Series: Hip-hop artists | Includes online resources and index.
Identifiers: ISBN 9781532190186 (lib. bdg.) | ISBN 9781532176036 (ebook)
Subjects: LCSH: Cardi B, 1992- (Belcalis Marlenis Almánzar)--Juvenile literature. | Rap (Music)--Juvenile literature. | Songwriters--Juvenile literature. | Television personalities--Juvenile literature. | Actress--Juvenile literature.
Classification: DDC 782.421649--dc23

CONTENTS

A HISTORIC WIN

When Cardi B arrived at the Grammys in February 2019, she was guaranteed to catch everyone's attention. Her fitted black-and-pink gown fanned out at her waist and made her look like a pink satin flower. She wore strings of pearls at her waist, around her neck, and in her hair. Some spectators thought she looked like a pearl in a clamshell. Surrounded by her entourage, it was impossible not to notice her walking into the Staples Center in Los Angeles, California. But the red carpet was only the first of Cardi's eye-catching moments that night.

The opening performance of the ceremony was Cardi's song "Money." The stage was designed to look like a plush couch with four tiers. The piano was covered in sparkles. A concert pianist started with a smooth, twinkling tune. Then a beat started, and the lights began flashing. Cardi appeared at the top of the stage in skin-tight leopard print

Cardi B posed on the red carpet at the Grammys in February 2019.

and sparkles. As she sang, she danced her way down the stage and climbed onto the piano like a jazz singer. When she stepped down from the piano, her dancers wrapped a peacock's tail of sheer black leopard print around her waist. The tail was similar to the shape of her gown on the red carpet. In classic Cardi fashion, her dancing, style, and sparkles kept everyone spellbound.

WHO IS CARDI B?

Cardi is one of very few female rap artists in a genre that is dominated by men. But that didn't stop her from taking over. She worked hard to rise from working as an exotic dancer in New York City's nightclubs to the top of the music industry. Her commercial debut album, *Invasion of Privacy*, was

MAKEUP ARTIST

Doing Cardi's makeup is a full-time job. Erika La' Pearl worked on the sets of *Love & Hip Hop: Atlanta* and *Real Housewives of Atlanta* before she was contacted to develop a cosmetic line with Cardi. She asked instead to be Cardi's makeup artist and has been working with her since 2016. The two have a close relationship. Cardi is La' Pearl's only client. She sometimes even does Cardi's makeup while the rapper sleeps. It adds an extra challenge for La' Pearl, but she is happy to do it so Cardi can be well rested.

Cardi B, *right*, climbed onto the piano while performing "Money."

released in April 2018, less than three years after she stopped working at nightclubs. The album rose to the top of the charts immediately. She has also released more than 25 separate singles.[1]

After her Grammy performance, Cardi took a seat in
the audience for the rest of the ceremony. When she was
announced the winner of the Grammy for Best Rap Album,
she was clearly surprised. Cardi was the first woman to
win the award for her solo work. She was so excited she

jumped up and down in her seat, the long fringes of her white gown and matching gloves flying. She hugged her husband, rapper Offset, who helped her to the stage.

At the microphone, she was barely able to breathe. Cardi went from crying to laughing and back as she thanked those who helped her with her album. She explained that the reason she finished the album on schedule was because she learned that she was pregnant. She wanted to film the music videos before she was obviously pregnant. That meant she had to hurry to finish writing and recording the music. Even though it meant some stressful months, Cardi thanked her baby daughter, Kulture Kiari, for motivating her to do it.

After the ceremony, in a dressing room and still wearing her fringed gown,

WOMEN AND THE GRAMMYS

The music industry is not always an easy place for women to succeed. In 2018, no women were nominated for the Grammy Award for Record of the Year, and only one woman was nominated for Album of the Year. But in 2019, five of the eight nominees for Album of the Year were female artists, including Cardi B. Brandi Carlile was the most nominated female artist with six nominations. Cardi was close to the top with five nominations, and she was the only female artist nominated for Best Rap Album.

A ROCKY MARRIAGE

For those who know Cardi, the biggest surprise on the Grammys red carpet was that her husband, rap artist Offset, was with her. Only a couple of months before, they had announced they were taking a break from their relationship. It was only at the Grammys that it became public that they were back together. When Cardi thanked Offset during her acceptance speech, some of the audience laughed. They weren't sure whether it was a joke, since their relationship had so recently been struggling. Cardi was sincere in her thanks, though. She appreciated that Offset pushed her to succeed.

"Five years ago I was still working hard, just like I'm working today, but I envisioned so little for myself. I settled for so much less."[2]

– *Cardi B*

Cardi posted a video to her Instagram account. In the video she was with her sister, her choreographer, her husband, and several members of her entourage. The shock may have worn off, but the excitement still hadn't. At one point in the video, the whole room started screaming and jumping up and down with excitement.

Cardi shouted more thanks for support to family and friends. She declared she would share the award with Mac Miller, who had been nominated for the same award and who had died the previous year.

Cardi's Grammy win came only two years after she officially entered the music industry. In those same two years, she did more than sign a record deal. She also got married, had a baby, recorded a hit album, filmed music videos, broke several records for women in rap and music, started a fashion line, and made time to speak out on national issues. A lot happened for Cardi in those years, and her life changed dramatically. There was no sign in 2019 that she planned to stop anytime soon.

LAURYN HILL

One other woman has won the Grammy for Best Rap Album. In 1998, Lauryn Hill won as a member of the group The Fugees. That year, Hill also became the only solo female rapper to reach Number 1 on the charts with her song "Doo-Wop (That Thing)." Because Hill shared the Grammy with her bandmates Wyclef Jean and Pras Michel, Cardi remained the only solo female to win it as of 2019. Cardi respects Hill's work, though. She had to get permission to reference Hill's music in her song "Be Careful." Cardi said that once Hill approved the reference, nobody could disapprove of the reference in her track.

COMING UP CARDI

Cardi was born on October 11, 1992. She grew up in the Highbridge neighborhood of the Bronx in New York City, New York. Her father is Dominican and has a strong sense of humor. Cardi's mother is Trinidadian and very serious. Cardi has 36 cousins, and her family is very close. Her parents separated when she was 13, so Cardi grew up living with her mom, but she still visited her dad and his family. She was always especially close to her grandmother, who Cardi says is the funniest in the family. Cardi's grandmother lived in Washington Heights, a Latin American neighborhood in Manhattan. Even once she had her own apartment, Cardi still said that her grandmother's house was her happy place. She would visit her grandmother often.

Cardi B is close to her sister, Hennessy Carolina, *right*.

The Washington Heights neighborhood, where Cardi's grandmother lived, is next to the George Washington Bridge in Manhattan.

CARDI'S EARLY YEARS

When she was born, Cardi's parents named her Belcalis Marlenis Almánzar. Cardi's sister, who is also a rising celebrity, is Hennessy Carolina. Because Hennessy is

a well-known brand of alcohol, people started calling

Belcalis "Bacardi," after a brand of rum. That turned into

"Cardi B." According to Cardi, "The 'B' stands for whatever,

depending on the day . . . beautiful or bully."[1]

When she was little, Cardi had severe asthma that sometimes kept her in the hospital for days or weeks. Cardi had a special machine called a nebulizer at home to help her breathe, but it made her shake. Her mother worried about her health. Because of her asthma, and because her mom didn't want her getting into trouble, Cardi wasn't allowed to go out often. She couldn't sleep over at friends' houses or go to parties. Looking back, Cardi admitted that if she had been allowed to go out as much as she wanted to, "I probably would be dead or got my face cut up. Or been a teenage mom."[2] As an adult, Cardi says she and her mother have a good relationship, even though "she gets a little spicy and I get a little spicy back."[3]

Cardi attended Renaissance High School

CARDI'S ACCENT

Both of Cardi's parents immigrated to the United States. She grew up speaking Spanish first and then English. Cardi's father only speaks to her in Spanish. Cardi also speaks with a dialect called African American Vernacular English (AAVE), which is associated with African American neighborhoods and with the hip-hop industry. Even though many people like her distinct accent, Cardi worries about it in her music. She says speaking English as a second language means she spends a lot of time "trying to pronounce words properly and without an accent" when she is recording.[4] She sometimes asks people to help make sure her lyrics make sense.

for Musical Theatre and Technology in the Bronx. English was one of her favorite subjects. In an interview, she said she loves the books *To Kill a Mockingbird* and *Their Eyes Were Watching God*. She also described herself as a "very rebellious teenager."[5] Since she wasn't allowed to go to parties at night, she cut school to party during the day with other students. As a result, she didn't do very well in school. After high school, Cardi took some classes at Manhattan Community College. However, she did not have the time or money to finish a degree, so she dropped out.

When Cardi was around 18 years old, her mother kicked her out of the house. Cardi ended up living with

"I LIKE IT" FEATURING BAD BUNNY AND J BALVIN

Given her heritage, it is fitting that Cardi's second single to hit Number 1 on the charts includes Spanish. "I Like It" features two other artists, J Balvin and Bad Bunny, who rap entirely in Spanish. The song samples a 1967 song of the same name by Pete Rodriguez, a Latin artist from the Bronx. "I Like It" is among an increasing number of Spanish-language songs topping the charts. Latin-style music has made it onto the charts often, but songs sung in Spanish rarely do. By the time "I Like It" was released in 2018, only three songs sung mostly or entirely in Spanish had ever reached the *Billboard* Top 10, but the number reaching the Top 100 continues to grow every year. "I Like It" was special for another reason. In July 2018, the song becoming Number 1 on the Hot 100 chart made Cardi B the first female rapper to have two Number 1 hits.

her boyfriend in his mom's house. Cardi's asthma flared up there and she had trouble breathing. Additionally, her boyfriend's sister used to steal money that Cardi earned from her job at a local Amish market. Perhaps worst of all, her boyfriend would beat her up. But Cardi didn't know where else to go. She didn't want to go back to her mom's house because she didn't want to admit she had no choice. Still, Cardi struggled and often went hungry.

GANG LIFE

Cardi joined a gang when she was 16 but stopped spending time with other gang members when she started dancing. She was focused on making money. Cardi says she doesn't talk about her affiliation much because she doesn't want people, especially young women, to think it's a good idea to join. Some critics say that if Cardi were really a member of a gang, she would have said something sooner. Cardi insists that if she had talked about her gang early on, she would never have gotten a record deal.

CARDI'S NEW JOB

After only a few months working at the market in 2011, Cardi was fired for giving too many discounts to her coworkers. She was terrified and didn't know where else to find a job. A manager told Cardi she should go work across the street in a nightclub as a dancer. Cardi was embarrassed and unsure she wanted to do that because it would mean taking off her clothes in front of strangers. Cardi's boss told her that being a dancer didn't mean she would have sex for money. He was able to get her a job as a dancer. Suddenly, Cardi could make as much in a single night of work as she had made in a week as a cashier at the market.

At first, Cardi was embarrassed about her new job. Even though she made a lot more money dancing, she says, "I imagined my mother shaking her head."[6] For the first two years she was dancing, Cardi told her family she made money babysitting for wealthy families. She promised herself she would quit dancing by the time she turned 25, but in the meantime, she saved as much money as she could. By the time she was 21, Cardi says she had saved roughly $20,000. Her plan was to save enough money to buy a house and make money renting it out.

Even though dancing and working in a club might sound like fun to some, the job is extremely

MANICURES

Cardi B's long, glamorously decorated fingernails are iconic. Her manicurist, Jenny Bui, has been working with Cardi for many years. Now that Cardi is famous, Bui has a private room in the back of her shop so that Cardi can have her nails done in peace. She does Cardi's nails about once a month, sometimes in her shop, sometimes flying out to meet Cardi wherever she is.

Some nightclubs hire dancers, who make money by dancing onstage for tips.

difficult and sometimes dangerous. In many places, like the businesses Cardi worked in, the dancers have to pay a "house fee" in order to work each day. If they don't make enough money to cover that fee, they go home with less money than when they started their shift. The customers at clubs are also often intoxicated, and they can become dangerous. Many clubs have a security team, but there is still a risk. Cardi saw her coworkers hit and abused by customers. For many clubs and the people who work in them, this is seen as a normal risk of the job.

> "Always have a goal, always have a second plan. Because in every field, whether it's dancing or something else, you gotta work hard for it."[8]
>
> – *Cardi B*

Security also can't stop customers from being rude, racist, or otherwise insulting to the dancers. Cardi has admitted that she cried when people told her she would never be anything but a dancer.

But dancing did have a silver lining for Cardi. She was making more money than she ever thought she would. Even though the job could be difficult, she says, "it also lifted my spirits when I needed some lifting."[7] She said later that she felt like her time there helped her to grow

DRUGGING MEN

In 2019, an Instagram video resurfaced of Cardi admitting to having drugged and robbed men while she worked as a dancer. Immediately, some people compared her to artist R. Kelly and actor Bill Cosby—men who were accused of using their celebrity status to drug and sexually assault women. In response, Cardi posted an explanation and apology in a since-deleted Instagram post. She wanted people to know she "made the choices that [she] did at the time because [she] had very limited options."[9] She continued,

> I was blessed to have been able to rise from that but so many women have not. . . . I'm a part of a hip-hop culture where you can . . . talk about the wrong things you had to do to get where you are. There are rappers that glorify murder, violence, drugs, [and] robbing. Crimes they feel they had to do to survive.[10]

Cardi added that she has never written about these incidents in her music, saying, "I'm not proud of it and feel a responsibility not to glorify it."[11]

up. The other women there also taught her to focus on making money. Now that she was making so much more than the market had been paying her, Cardi was able to move out of her boyfriend's house and escape her abusive relationship. She says that dancing in the club saved her life but that it's not something she would recommend for anyone else.

THE PRESSURE TO CHANGE

Besides it being dangerous and exhausting, Cardi explained in an interview that the job also hurt her self-image. She liked the way she looked until she

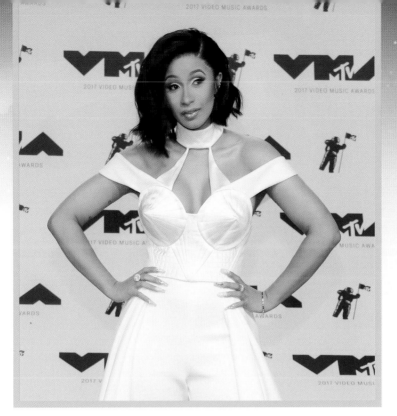

Cardi B is open about her struggles with her body image.

started dancing. Seeing all the women around her who looked different, Cardi felt like she had to change the way she looked in order to make money.

She traveled to the Dominican Republic to have breast augmentation surgery. She also visited a woman's home in Queens to have injections to make her butt bigger. Although this sort of procedure is not uncommon, it is very dangerous. Cardi could have gotten an infection and been left permanently scarred. Having unidentified synthetic materials injected into her body could have

Cardi B felt pressured to change her appearance when she worked as a dancer.

killed her. It was extremely painful, and the injections leaked for almost a week afterward. She has also admitted that she still doesn't know what's in her body. She regrets the injections because she had them before her body was entirely done growing. She was only 22, and since then her body changed so that now she feels like her butt is too big.

Her years as a dancer had a big impact on Cardi's life, but they didn't make her who she is. She knew she never wanted to dance for the rest of her life, and she was determined to make as much money as she could and get out of the business. After four years dancing in clubs, Cardi found a way to make a living elsewhere.

SOCIAL MEDIA FAME

In 2013, Cardi started posting short videos to social media. She became extremely popular. People liked her bright personality and the content she posted. "People just like my voice . . . or something," Cardi said.[1] In just a few years, she became a minor celebrity in New York. According to Cardi, she doesn't play a character on social media; she just shows who she is.

One of her most famous posts was a video clip of her wearing a strappy bralette and a short skirt. According to the short video, Cardi says she is "still looking like a thotty" even though it is winter "because a hoe never gets cold!"[2] Soon Cardi B had over one million followers on social media and had a manager who helped her find new gigs. She had grown her brand so much that she quit her shifts as a dancer, working her last shift on her birthday, October 11, 2015.

Cardi B says that she became famous on social media because of her personality and her smile.

SPEECH PATTERNS

Cardi is also famous for the way she speaks. She has a New York accent, but she took her language a step further with her own sounds. "Okurrr" means "okay" but ends in a trilled 'r' sound, "like a cold pigeon." She says "eeeoooowwww," which she once explained as "a sad cat sound," when something is good news.[3] In 2019, Cardi trademarked "okurrr." Only her brand or those with her permission can use the word on clothing or merchandise.

> "I was always scared to follow my dreams because if I follow my dreams and I fail, I can't dream about it anymore."[4]
>
> – *Cardi B*

NEW OPPORTUNITIES

Because she was so popular, Cardi was invited to join the show *Love & Hip Hop: New York* in 2015. The reality television show focuses on people who are on the edge of the music industry: artists, producers, managers, DJs, and their families and close friends. Cardi wasn't known as a rap artist at the time, but she was writing music. At first, Cardi wasn't sure about joining the show. Even though she is honest on social media, she is still careful about what she makes public. She didn't want to put her entire life on television, and she was worried the show would ruin her reputation. She didn't want to be a reality TV star; she wanted to focus on her music.

Eventually, Cardi agreed to join *Love & Hip Hop* because it paid well and would provide a lot of publicity. She introduced herself to the audience saying, "You might know me as that annoying dancer on social media . . . but I'm just a regular, degular, shmegular girl from the Bronx."[5] In one of her first episodes on *Love & Hip Hop*, Cardi found out the man she was seeing had another girlfriend. The two women got into a fight, and later, Cardi explained what happened. Turning away from the camera mid-sentence and then dramatically back, she said, "If a girl have beef with me, she gon' have beef with me . . . foreva."[6] This became an iconic moment for her on the show and inspired her song "Foreva" on her first mixtape, *Gangsta B**** Music, Vol. 1*.

Before starting on *Love & Hip Hop*, Cardi's manager had suggested she pursue

BEING MARY JANE

Shortly after leaving *Love & Hip Hop*, Cardi made an appearance on an episode of the BET drama *Being Mary Jane* in 2017. She played an over-the-top reality TV star named Mercedes who wasn't much different from the real Cardi. At first, Mercedes and Mary Jane do not talk using the same slang or dialect. However, when they get into an argument, Mary Jane's accent shifts to match Mercedes'. This is sometimes called "code-switching." People of color often feel like they have to learn to speak differently depending on who is listening. Characters on the show talk about having to code-switch in order to be successful in journalism.

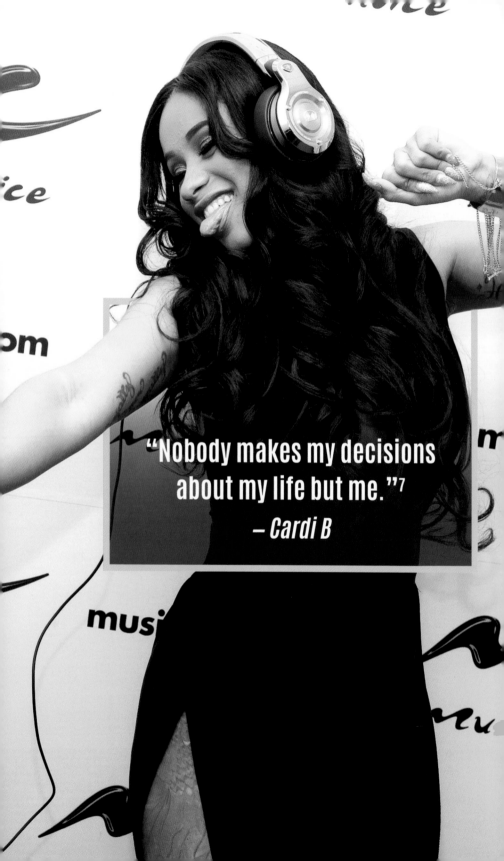

"Nobody makes my decisions about my life but me."[7]
– *Cardi B*

Shortly after releasing her first mixtape, Cardi visited Music Choice, which creates music channels for cable television.

rapping, but Cardi was unsure. Even once she became successful in music, Cardi insisted that her priority was making money. In those early years, however, she was even more concerned about being able to succeed and pay her bills. With all the thousands of people in New York who wanted to be rappers, she asked, "What makes me think that out of all of them I'm going to make it?"[8] Although she was worried about putting too much time and money into something that might fail, she did start writing more music during her time on the show.

THE BEGINNING OF HER MUSIC CAREER

In March 2016, Cardi released her first mixtape, *Gangsta B**** Music, Vol. 1*. At this point, she didn't have a contract with a record label, but she did work with KSR Group. KSR is a talent management company that works with independent artists. It organized an 11-city tour for several of its clients in the summer of 2016 with Cardi as the headliner. That fall, it also released a mixtape to commemorate the tour, called *Underestimated: The Album*. Cardi had three solo tracks on the album and three more songs that she performed with others.

HENNESSY CAROLINA

Cardi's sister Hennessy Carolina is only three years younger than Cardi, and the two are very close. Hennessy was invited onto *Love & Hip Hop* in 2016 as a guest. When Cardi decided she was leaving the show, Hennessy became a supporting member of the cast. She also has a contract with KSR Group as an independent artist, and in 2018 she was a part of the Milan Fashion Show. Hennessy faced a challenge when she decided to tell her traditional Caribbean family about her girlfriend. Although her family was unhappy at first, Hennessy was able to convince them that "love is love no matter what gender."[9]

"Everybody wanna be famous but, like, people don't realize being famous don't make you like rich. Like, yo you really gotta work to get rich."[10]

– *Cardi B*

While the stars of *Love & Hip Hop* become nationally known, they don't always have the time to push their own music. Cardi's tour and first mixtape happened while she was on the show. But in December 2016, Cardi announced she was leaving the show to focus on her music.

Cardi doesn't want people to think that it was *Love & Hip Hop* that made her a rapper. She wrote songs before joining the show, but they weren't ready to be released yet. Within just a few months of leaving the show, though, Cardi signed a multimillion-dollar deal with Atlantic Records. Cardi hit the ground running on

In her last few months on *Love & Hip Hop*, Cardi appeared in *Vibe Viva*, a digital publication from *Vibe* magazine.

June 16, 2017, with her commercial debut single "Bodak Yellow." The song started at Number 85 on the *Billboard* charts and eventually made its way up to Number 1. It was only the second time in history a solo female rapper topped the charts.

Two of Cardi's next few songs were collaborations with other artists. She and A$AP Rocky were both featured on G-Eazy's song "No Limit," which reached Number 4 on the charts. The following month, Cardi and Nicki Minaj

Cardi B won Hustler of the Year at the 2017 BET Hip Hop Awards.

were featured on a song by Migos called "MotorSport," which reached Number 6. On October 10, 2017, Cardi was the most-nominated woman at the BET Hip Hop Awards. She took home five awards—the most of any artist that night. Within six months of signing her deal, Cardi B's first three songs reached the top ten. This had only been achieved by two other artists—R&B singer Ashanti and the rock group the Beatles. Cardi was taking the industry by storm.

BILLBOARD CHARTS

Billboard has been publishing music charts for more than 80 years. They measure how popular a song or album is based on how many times it is purchased or played during a week. The Hot 100 is a list of the most popular songs, while the *Billboard* 200 lists the most popular albums. There are also charts that look at just one kind of music, like pop or country. Some nations even have separate charts. *Billboard* charts have been used as a mark of success in the music industry for decades.

FAMILY AND RELATIONSHIPS

Cardi B's wedding wasn't quite what fans might have expected. She was married the same day her boyfriend, rapper Offset, proposed to her, on September 20, 2017. Instead of a big white dress, she wore a white tracksuit. Instead of a tuxedo, her husband wore jeans and a black sweatshirt. Instead of all their friends and family, only one of Cardi's cousins was there as a witness. There wasn't even a wedding ring. The two kept their marriage a secret for nearly half a year.

CARDI AND OFFSET

When Cardi first started dating Offset at the beginning of 2017, she was protective of the relationship. She worried that if they announced it to the world, people would interfere or even try to break them up. So they kept it to themselves for a few weeks. They collaborated on her

Cardi B and her husband, Offset, kept their relationship a secret until late 2017.

single "Lick" in January 2017, and the next month they went to the Super Bowl together. Once the two of them appeared together in public, Cardi knew there would be a lot of eyes on them. She didn't want to look foolish for dating a man who was not faithful to her. She asked her publicist, Patience Foster, to make sure Offset was serious about their relationship.

Over the next few months, Cardi didn't directly admit to dating Offset. But even though they tried to fly under the radar, their fans were suspicious. By the summer, it was common knowledge that the two were together. Even though they were married in September, Offset proposed publicly to Cardi during one of her concerts in Philadelphia, Pennsylvania, in October. She thanked him later for trying to make sure she had that special moment in front of the world.

WHO IS OFFSET?

Offset is a member of the Atlanta, Georgia, rap group Migos. His groupmates are his cousin Takeoff and Takeoff's uncle, Quavo. Their 2013 song "Versace" made it onto the Top 100. Since then, they have had over 30 songs on the charts. In 2019, at the age of 27, Offset released his debut solo album, *Father of 4*. He continued to work with Quavo and Takeoff as part of one of the most popular rap groups in the music scene.

In January 2018, playing along with the official reports that she wasn't married yet, Cardi announced her wedding would be pushed back. She said she and Offset were both too busy for the weeks-long type of wedding she wanted. Both of them were planning tours and putting out new albums. Some fans didn't accept this excuse and thought Cardi might be pregnant, but she refused to confirm the rumor.

That summer, tabloid news organization TMZ found a copy of a marriage certificate between Cardi and Offset dated September 2017. Cardi was frustrated that TMZ announced it publicly, but there was nothing she could do. She said that was the sort of thing that made her name her album

"I'd seen her potential, her vision, her grind. Whatever she does, she's going to master it. She's like me."[1]

— Offset

A PUBLIC ANNOUNCEMENT

In April 2018, Cardi publicly announced her pregnancy on *Saturday Night Live*. For her first performance of the night, she wore a feathery costume that hid her stomach from view. Near the end of the show, she performed her soulful song "Be Careful" in a fitted white gown. The crowd cheered as her "baby bump" came into view. Afterward, she said on Instagram, "I'm finally free!" because she didn't have to hide herself now that everyone knew about the pregnancy.[2]

Offset, *right*, said he was too busy touring with Migos to get married. However, he and Cardi B had already been married in secret.

Invasion of Privacy, because "people will do the most to be nosey about your life." She explained that getting married was a moment "that I want[ed] to keep for myself."[3]

PREGNANCY

In a 2015 interview, Cardi said she wanted to have a child
by the time she was 25. But she also wanted to have a

FIGHTING DEPRESSION

When Cardi's pregnancy became public, a lot of people started telling her she wouldn't be able to continue her career with a baby. Even though she didn't plan to quit, the pressure to quit working and the stress of pregnancy weighed on her. When Kulture was born, Cardi's doctor told her about postpartum depression, a mood disorder that sometimes affects women shortly after giving birth. Cardi thought it wouldn't be a problem for her, "but out of nowhere, the world was heavy on my shoulders."[4] Thanks in part to her family's help, she started to feel better a few months after the baby was born.

career. Other people in the industry told her it would ruin her career to have a baby. When she became pregnant, Cardi did not make it public. Instead, she worked long hours to make sure her album would be finished before she had her baby.

Cardi didn't publicly announce her pregnancy for several months. It still took a toll on her body, though. In April 2018, she announced she was canceling the rest of her tour because she had trouble breathing. Some people experience shortness of breath during pregnancy. That could make it hard for anyone to sing and dance, and Cardi already had asthma. Cardi was so successful at hiding her pregnancy, there were rumors that the reason she canceled her performances was so she could prepare to be in a movie. It wasn't much longer until she officially told everyone she was pregnant.

Cardi B says that Kulture is with her all of the time—unless she's getting her signature nails done.

On July 10, 2018, Cardi's daughter Kulture Kiari was born. Cardi had planned to go on tour with Bruno Mars two months later. Initially, she expected to take the baby with her. She later said she "underestimated this mommy thing" and canceled her plans so she could stay home longer.[5] Since then, she has managed to keep Kulture with her through much of her work. According to Cardi, the "only time I don't have my baby with me is when I'm getting my hair done, makeup done, performing."[6]

Initially, Cardi and Offset did not release pictures of their baby to the public. Some people said that was because the child must be ugly, and this made

KULTURE KIARI

According to Cardi, Offset chose the name for their daughter: Kulture Kiari. Offset's legal name is Kiari Kendrell Cephus, so not only does his daughter have his name but they also have the same initials. When Cardi was pregnant, the two most recent albums from Offset's rap group Migos were called *Culture* and *Culture II*. Fans quickly noticed the connection with his music and the baby's new name. Kulture also has three older half siblings from her father's previous relationships.

Offset angry. He wanted to post a photo to show off his daughter, but the family also received threats of violence. The couple certainly didn't want to endanger their child or themselves. After several months of back and forth, Cardi posted a picture of Kulture in a baby carrier to Instagram so the family could stop trying to hide their baby every time they left the house.

SPLIT WITH OFFSET

Off and on throughout their marriage, there had been rumors that Offset was cheating on Cardi. More of these rumors surfaced not long after Kulture was born. In December 2018, Cardi announced on Instagram that she and her husband were splitting up, though she didn't say that they were definitely getting divorced. Even though they still loved each other, things weren't working out.

Cardi insisted they were still good friends. In another video, she expressed her thanks for all Offset taught her about the music industry. Offset didn't directly admit to cheating on Cardi, but he did apologize on Instagram for "partaking in activity that I shouldn't have been partaking in."[7]

Some said the two weren't really breaking up and that Cardi was just trying to get attention. She insisted that wasn't true. Both she and Offset had their own careers and an infant daughter to worry about. "Think we want to put our life out there for what?" she asked on Instagram. "What we gain from publicity? Nothing."[8] There was too much for them to worry about without creating more drama for themselves.

FAMILY AND MUSIC

Cardi doesn't forget her daughter when she's working. In the fall of 2018, Cardi released her single "Money," the first since Kulture was born. The song is about money and luxury items, but the music video also features Cardi breastfeeding her daughter. In the last refrain of the chorus, one line changes. She says there's "nothing in this world that I like more than Kulture."[9] At this point in her Grammy performance of the song, she even flashed a heart sign with her hands.

"Ain't no type of publicity that I would ever want that would have my daughter looking at me crazy when she gets older."[10]
– Cardi B

Cardi B and Offset performed together during his set at Revolve Festival in April 2019.

Cardi said she already didn't get to spend enough time with her family because she worked so much.

Only a couple months after they announced their separation, Offset and Cardi went to the Grammy Awards together in February 2019. Despite the ups and downs

of their relationship, Cardi said in an interview that she appreciates the support Offset provides. He encouraged her to spend time in the studio and not to be afraid to make her own decisions.

PUBLIC REPUTATION

Cardi says she got into fights often when she was young because of her big personality. She also credits her neighborhood with teaching her to, as she says, "pop off."[1] As with everything else about her, Cardi does not filter her fighting personality. She fought with several people, verbally and physically, during her rise to fame.

During a *Love & Hip Hop* reunion episode in 2017, Cardi argued with one of her costars, Asia. "You judged me because I was a stripper! Say the truth!" Cardi shouted.[2] The security guards didn't realize Cardi was taking off her shoe until she threw it at Asia. Cardi's sister, Hennessy, then charged at Asia. Cardi followed her, but both were tackled by security.

On August 29, 2018, only a month after Kulture was born, Cardi and her entourage were at a local club. There were rumors that Offset had cheated on Cardi with one of

In April 2019, Cardi B rejected a plea deal over charges that she ordered her bodyguards to attack two bartenders.

the bartenders there. In the early morning, members of Cardi's team started throwing objects at the bartenders.

Cardi was accused of throwing chairs and bottles. Her legal team insisted that she didn't throw anything and that it was all the people around her.

As a result of this incident, Cardi was charged with one count of assault and two counts of reckless endangerment. Both are significant misdemeanors. Cardi did not attend her first court date, saying her schedule was too busy. The prosecutor asked for a warrant to be put out for her arrest, but the judge gave her one more chance to show up for court. When she finally appeared in court in December, the

> "I was always a pretty girl and always mad-hype so everyone wanted to fight me so I had to fight them back."[3]
>
> – Cardi B

CARDI'S BODYGUARDS

In May 2018, Cardi was leaving the Met Gala just after 2:00 a.m. when a stranger asked her for an autograph. She said no and attempted to walk away, but the man kept insisting. Video was later released showing the man being beat up by three others. The man was kept in the hospital overnight to make sure there was nothing wrong. In the end, they didn't find any significant injuries. Nonetheless, the police sought the men who had committed the assault, two of whom were Cardi's bodyguards.

prosecutor asked that Cardi be required to post bail to go home. The judge disagreed because Cardi was not a flight risk, meaning that she wouldn't flee and try to avoid her court date. He did tell Cardi not to contact the bartenders either online or in person. Cardi was offered a plea deal for the incident. If she pleaded guilty to one of the charges, she could be released instead of going to jail for up to a year. In April 2019, she rejected the deal.

CARDI'S CREW

As boisterous as Cardi can be in her own defense, sometimes it is the people she has grown close to who are first to defend her. Shortly after Cardi announced that she and Offset were separating, a fan told Cardi it must be because she was so rude. Cardi's publicist, Patience Foster, jumped to Cardi's defense, threatening to "smack the s***" out of the fan.[4] Although there was no physical assault, some people didn't like the way Foster handled the situation. Foster saw no reason to apologize for defending her friend and employer, though. Cardi publicly announced her support for Foster as well.

Foster stepped in to try to help Cardi on another occasion as well. When Cardi and Offset first separated, the publicist hoped to bring the two back together.

Patience Foster, *left*, defends Cardi B as both her friend and her publicist.

She brought Offset to the stage during one of Cardi's performances. Offset interrupted Cardi's performance to tell her he was sorry. Neither Cardi nor her fans appreciated the gesture, but Foster was just trying to help. Cardi again defended her friend over the incident.

FEUD WITH NICKI MINAJ

Cardi's best-known and longest-running feud has been with rap artist Nicki Minaj. Many people have compared Minaj and Cardi throughout Cardi's career. Women in rap are rare, and both artists are of Afro-Caribbean descent. They are strong women who use their sexuality to work their ways through a male-dominated industry. The two were both featured on the song "MotorSport" by Migos in 2017, but even then, they were not close friends. A few months before, a screenshot made it look as though Nicki Minaj had "liked" a comment on Instagram that insulted some of Cardi's lyrics. Some people believed it was Photoshopped. The two insisted they were not fighting, though, and Minaj even congratulated Cardi when "Bodak Yellow" hit Number 1 on the charts.

PATIENCE FOSTER

Patience Foster, Cardi's publicist, has been an entrepreneur since middle school, when she sold her own magazine to other students. After college, she decided her job wasn't paying her enough, so she quit and opened her own salon not long after her son was born. Though her business was a success, at age 26 she got a job in public relations. While she was working as an unpaid intern, she met Cardi's manager at a fashion show. Foster became Cardi's publicist, and the two have become very protective of each other over the years.

"You know a lot of people like to say all publicity is good publicity but to me it's not because that takes away people paying attention to your craft. It makes people not even care about your craft. They just want to see drama."[5]

— Cardi B

Nicki Minaj and Cardi B have been feuding throughout Cardi B's career.

In 2018, Cardi accused Minaj of threatening to not work with other artists if they worked with Cardi. During New York Fashion Week in September 2018, Cardi left a party barefoot. Video later appeared online showing Cardi inside the building throwing a shoe at Minaj. Security guards stopped Cardi from reaching Minaj. In the process, one of them may have hit Cardi with an elbow. By the time she was escorted out, she had a lump on her forehead. She later posted on Instagram that despite tensions between them, Cardi had only started to fight when Minaj insulted her parenting. Minaj denied that she ever said anything about Cardi's daughter.

There were many prominent people in the fashion and entertainment industries at the event. Minaj said in an interview

"MOTORSPORT" CONTROVERSY

Cardi claimed in an interview that Minaj rewrote her verse in "MotorSport" after she found out she would be working with Cardi, implying that Minaj was intimidated. Minaj was upset by this and said Cardi had begged to be on the song. Some people speculated that Cardi and Minaj's parts in the video for "MotorSport" were filmed separately because Minaj and Cardi didn't want to work together. Minaj also accused Cardi of not showing enough gratitude for getting to work with her. Early in her career, Minaj had also been accused of not showing gratitude to Lil' Kim, who helped her rise to stardom.

that fighting in front of them was very embarrassing.
Cardi wasn't embarrassed, but she did admit that it was
unnecessary and bad for business. Their feud continued
through social media for several weeks. Both launched
fashion lines in the following months, and this only
increased the competition. In October, Minaj posted
that she wanted to only focus on positive things, not
the fighting and drama. Cardi agreed, but that didn't mean the rest of the world was ready to forget their rivalry.

When Cardi took home a Grammy for *Invasion of Privacy*, BET posted a rude comment about Minaj, who had also been nominated for the award. Mary J. Blige, a longtime R&B artist and actress, spoke out against the attempt to pit the two rappers against each other. She noted how hard it can

MINAJ'S CANCELED CONCERT

In March 2019, Minaj canceled a
performance in France the day of
the event. The star said that the
venue did not have the proper
electricals for her performance.
Minaj's fans were not happy.
By the time the concert was
canceled, some people were
already in the venue. They
started chanting "Cardi B." They
knew the two stars did not get
along. Minaj apologized to her
fans and said there had been
miscommunication between her
team and the venue about the
building. She insisted she hadn't
wanted to cancel the show either.

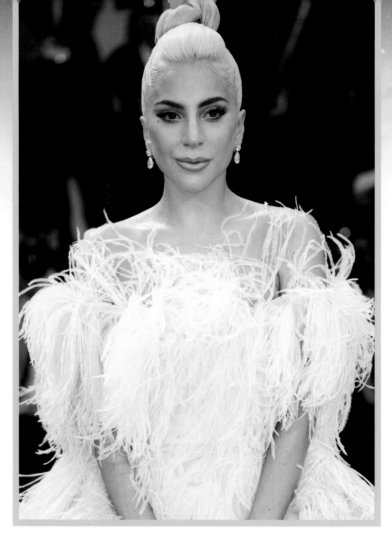

Lady Gaga believes that Cardi B and all women face challenges in the music industry.

be for women to succeed in the music industry. "At least try to lift us up together," she added.[6] Cardi also rejected BET's comment, saying that putting one person down in order to lift someone else up isn't her style. BET deleted the comment and apologized that it was ever written.

Some people said Cardi did not deserve to win the award. Several stars stepped forward to defend her. Lady Gaga wrote on Twitter about the challenges faced by women in the music industry. She pointed out "how hard we work through the disrespectful challenges, just to make art."[7] Although Cardi initially posted a video of her angrily defending her win, she later deleted it. Instead, she described all the hard work that went into finishing the album on time. She explained she had slept in the studio for months. Once the album was finished, she still had to film music videos. She had dealt with migraines to finish the album before the last months of her pregnancy. In the end, the album was in the top ten for 21 weeks. Whatever some people might say, Cardi's hard work paid off.

Chapter Six

"TEN DIFFERENT LOOKS AND MY LOOKS ALL KILL"

D espite her success, Cardi has looked to branch out with her music style. In an interview she explained she wanted a smoother flow than she had on her mixtapes. She has also broken out of her box by collaborating with other artists and moving from music to other industries. She has partnered with several companies for advertising and designed her own eye shadow line. She has performed on *Saturday Night Live* and has both performed and served as a cohost on *The Tonight Show*. Her first Fashion Nova clothing line has brought her the most attention, though. When it first went on sale on November 15, 2018, it sold out in just a few hours.

Cardi B walked the red carpet at the release party of her Fashion Nova line in 2018.

Fashion Nova sells fast fashion clothing. Other fast fashion stores include H&M and Forever 21.

FASHION NOVA

Cardi didn't have experience in the fashion industry, but she did have a long relationship with the fast fashion company Fashion Nova. Much of Fashion Nova's popularity is due to celebrities modeling the company's clothing on social media. For example, Cardi is paid up

to $20,000 per month to advertise Fashion Nova on Instagram. The company produces many new items every week. As a result, they are able to sell new items only days after a celebrity is seen wearing them.

According to Cardi, Fashion Nova is one of the few companies that makes jeans that fit her distinctive curves.

> "Wanna know how rich people like me stay rich? By staying on a budget. These pants right here are Fashion Nova."[1]
>
> – *Cardi B*

Their prices also tend to be less than those of designer labels. Some people consider the price of an item to bring prestige, but Cardi is happy to spend $20 on a pair of jeans if they look good on her. She has become known for mixing high and low fashion pieces in her outfits, and her fashion is often mentioned in her songs. In "Money," she raps that she has "ten different

Cardi B wore a stunning red dress to the 2019 Met Gala where the theme was Camp: Notes on Fashion.

looks [outfits] and my looks all kill."[2] Her song "She Bad" even includes the line "I could buy designer, but this Fashion Nova fit."[3]

Many women considered "curvy" find it difficult to find well-fitting clothing in certain stores. According to Cardi, women of color struggle the most with this. Her own experience struggling to find clothing that fit her properly affected her plans for her own fashion line. She wanted a line that would be inclusive of curvy women like her. In an interview with *Elle*, she said her pet peeve is jeans that gap at the waist, which is usually a result of clothes made for less-curvy people. The real challenge for Cardi's line was to design clothing that would look good on people of all shapes. Cardi worked hard to make sure her fashion line would be a success.

THE TONIGHT SHOW

Cardi has served as cohost to Jimmy Fallon on *The Tonight Show*, as well as performed on the show several times. In April 2018, she joined Fallon to talk, interview other guests, and perform. "I'm the first late night cohost that isn't a white guy!" she said.[4] The guest of the show that night was comedian John Mulaney. The three discussed babies, because Cardi had just announced she was pregnant. They also talked about high school proms. Cardi said her boyfriend had broken up with her only weeks before her prom, but she managed to have a good prom night even without him.

Cardi designed more than 80 pieces with Fashion Nova for her first collection, most of which cost around $40 or less. They include suits, blouses, dresses, accessories, and jeans, and the sizes range from junior to curvy. She wanted her line to look like high-end fashion while still being affordable. Many of the items are designed to be worn in business settings while still showing off Cardi's style. She said, "I want women to feel rich, to feel like me. I didn't want to make it so 'hoochie mama.'"[5]

Cardi looked to high-end designers like Chanel, Yves Saint Laurent, and Dior when designing her pieces. She also worked with Fashion Nova to make sure the clothes they produced were made well from good materials. The clothes would have her name on them, so it was important to her that they be loved.

Her second Fashion Nova line released on May 8, 2019. Cardi described the collection on her Instagram as having

"a lot of fun colors, but it gets so *Matrix*, so sleek, so clean."
She added, "It's also very chic—not that thotty, though I
do got some thotty pieces, you know what I'm saying?"[6]
Cardi stressed that the
collection was for people of
all body types, whom she
said would look good in
her clothes.

OTHER BUSINESS ENDEAVORS

As a fan of shoes, Cardi
hopes to design a shoe line
one day. Her popularity
has helped more than one
company's sales. When she
mentioned Louboutin shoes
in her single "Bodak Yellow,"
searches for the brand more
than doubled. After she named Balenciagas in "I Like It,"
Fashion Nova started reproducing that company's style.
In 2018, she partnered with the shoe brand Reebok to
advertise a line of sneaker styles from the 1990s. Cardi
appeared in a commercial full of 1990s trends including

BLACKNESS

Cardi B identifies as black, but
she is often more vocal about her
Latin heritage. For her, race and
ethnicity do not have to cancel
each other out. In May 2018,
rapper Azealia Banks insulted
Cardi, calling her a "caricature
of a black woman."[7] Banks said
that if Nicki Minaj talked the way
Cardi did, nobody would support
Minaj. Cardi insisted she was true
to herself and intended to stay
that way. In an interview, she said
she is tired of people trying to
decide her race or heritage for
her based on what she looks like.

Louboutin shoes are known for their red soles. In "Bodak Yellow," Cardi B refers to her Louboutins, rapping, "these is red bottoms, these is bloody shoes."

COMPETING WITH MINAJ

Fashion became another field in which Cardi and Nicki Minaj could compete. In 2018, Minaj released a fashion line with the company Diesel. Cardi claimed she had been asked to partner with them first but had to turn it down. The CEO of Diesel denied Cardi's claim. Minaj then said she had been offered a contract with Fashion Nova. Cardi responded that everybody partners with Fashion Nova. After several days of back-and-forth on social media, Minaj and Cardi agreed to focus on the positives, rather than publicly fighting. Their truce lasted several months, until the Grammys.

the "Macarena" dance and slap bracelets.

Cardi's support can bring in a lot of money for companies. In 2018, fashion company Tom Ford named a shade of bright blue lipstick after her. The color was released shortly after Cardi threw a shoe at Nicki Minaj, so there was some worry about Tom Ford supporting the rapper. Even so, the lipstick sold out in 24 hours. The CEO of Fashion Nova said that Cardi's support helped validate the company. The clothing resale platform Poshmark said sales of Fashion Nova more than doubled when Cardi partnered with them.

Cardi appeared in several commercials aired during the Super Bowl. In 2018, she was in a commercial for

A few months before her Pepsi Super Bowl commercial, Cardi performed at the 2018 Pepsi Jingle Bash.

Amazon's digital voice assistant Alexa in which celebrities filled in when Alexa lost her voice. The following year, an ad for Pepsi showcased Cardi's way of speaking as people in a diner attempted to trill "okurrr." Cardi made an appearance in another Pepsi commercial with actor

Steve Carell. As "I Like It" plays, she enters a diner and drums her elaborately manicured nails on a bedazzled Pepsi can. Though perhaps not a sign that Cardi intends to go into acting, these ads are one sign of how popular she has become.

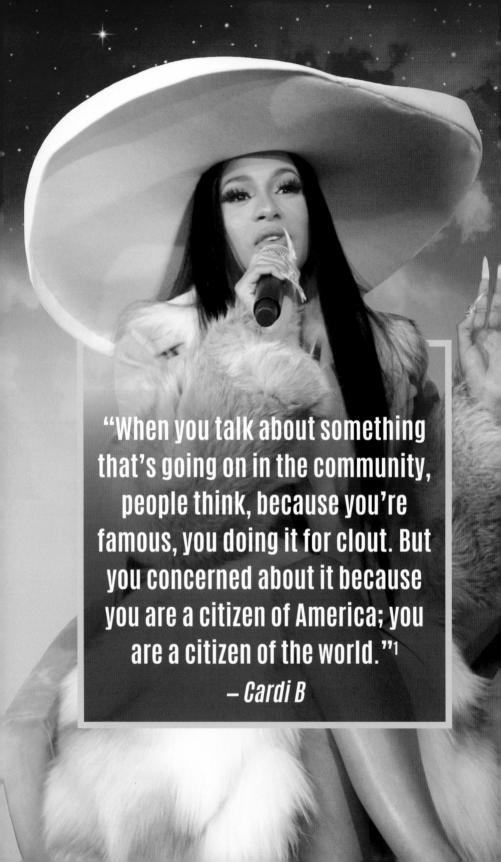

"When you talk about something that's going on in the community, people think, because you're famous, you doing it for clout. But you concerned about it because you are a citizen of America; you are a citizen of the world."[1]

– *Cardi B*

NOT AFRAID TO SPEAK UP

Cardi B was never a quiet person, and she is interested in politics. When she was taking college courses, she focused on history and political science, as well as French. She used to be able to name all of the US presidents in order, and her favorite was Franklin Delano Roosevelt. She pays close attention to current politics. It's frustrating to her that she is accused of speaking about political or social issues just for attention. Cardi considers being a citizen of the country and of the world reason enough to pay attention and be active.

Many male rappers brag about selling or doing drugs or breaking the law before they became famous. The reaction to Cardi's past is often different. Her work as a dancer was not illegal, but it is often used to insult or dismiss her. However, Cardi believes dancers should be treated with as much respect as any other entertainer.

Cardi B is not afraid to speak her mind when it comes to politics, fashion, and women in hip-hop, among other topics.

In January 2019, the video for City Girls' song "Twerk" featuring Cardi B was released. The video shows many women in bikinis twerking in different places. Journalist Stephanie Hamill suggested that the video objectified women rather than empowering them. Cardi responded that a woman's ability to choose how to dance is empowering. No matter what she is wearing or doing, Cardi said, "NO still means NO."[3]

She has never tried to hide her past. She continues to openly discuss her former job in part to remove the stigma against working as an exotic dancer.

FEMINISM AND THE #METOO MOVEMENT

Other people started calling Cardi a feminist before she did. One of the main ideas of feminism is that a woman should be able to choose her own path in life. Many people disagree on what feminism in action looks like. Cardi has been called a "hood feminist" because she does not fit the mold of a formally educated woman. She disagrees with the idea that only women with college degrees can be activists for women's rights. "That is not being a feminist," she said on Instagram.[2]

"If you don't support all women, then you're not a real feminist."[4]

– Cardi B

Some say Cardi can't be a feminist because she

is openly sexual. For them, women who make money from their appearance or their bodies are saying that a woman's worth is based on what she looks like. For Cardi, feminism means being able to choose what she wants to do with her body, and whether she wants to show it off or not. If she can make money that way, she says, then that is her choice.

The #MeToo movement took off in 2017 when female celebrities spoke up about their experiences with assault and sexual harassment. Other women soon joined in. Some shared their stories. Others only felt comfortable saying "me too." The number of women who came

The #MeToo movement became an international conversation about sexual harassment and assault.

ACCUSATIONS OF TRANSPHOBIA

Transphobia is the hatred or intolerance for transgender (trans) people, or people whose gender identity does not match the sex they were assigned at birth. Cardi has been accused of transphobia, particularly against trans women. Many people were angered when a video was posted online of her using offensive terms to refer to trans women. Cardi apologized for her language, saying she didn't realize it was offensive. Later, one of the same terms was posted on her Facebook page. She said that one of her assistants must have posted it, because she did not. Cardi insisted that she cares very much about LGBTQ rights, but some are not ready to forgive her for repeating the same mistake.

forward was shocking to many. The rise of the #MeToo movement brought sexual harassment and assault into common conversation. Cardi's experiences make her well positioned to discuss both. Female entertainers, whether they are working in clubs or in music videos, often experience abuse from customers and from those who hire and supervise them.

Cardi has argued that the #MeToo movement overlooks women who flaunt their sexuality, even when they are doing it to pay their bills. This is especially true of the women who dance in music videos. Sometimes called "video vixens," many are unheard even when they try to tell someone what happened to them. Before she was famous, Cardi struggled to get into music videos and was harassed in the process. She says these women are dismissed because they wear revealing clothing and flaunt their sexuality. Meanwhile, Cardi believes many of the men who run the industry and have expressed support for the movement are just as guilty of harassment. "They're not woke," Cardi B said, "they're scared [people will find out]."[5]

> **"Y'all going to respect these strippers from now on . . . Just because somebody was a stripper don't mean they don't have no brain."[6]**
>
> – *Cardi B*

Despite the people who disagree with her, Cardi is in a position to make an impact on the way women and girls see themselves. She is body positive and encourages people to value themselves, whatever they look like. This is one of the reasons she doesn't recommend being a dancer to anyone else. Before she started dancing, Cardi was happy with her appearance. When she got a job in a club, she started questioning her body. For dancers, looking a certain way can be the difference between enough money to pay bills and losing money during their shift. Cardi's self-image was worn down until she got plastic surgery. She was insulted for her body before her surgery and injections. Since then, she has been insulted for the way she looks and for having surgery. "People are

ORIENTALISM

In the music video for "Bodak Yellow," Cardi rides through the desert on a camel. She is with other people, and all of them are dressed in traditional Middle Eastern clothing. The video features a cheetah and women dancing with swords and fire. Cardi was accused of "orientalism." This is when European or North American people see all the different cultures of the Middle East or Asia as the same, and as either exotic or primitive. Usually this also carries the idea that the people living there are inferior. Some felt Cardi's video disrespected Middle Eastern and North African cultures by making them seem different and exotic. Others see the video as celebratory of these cultures. Because she is of African descent, some argue that she has a right to connect to her roots.

never satisfied," she said in an interview. "Why does it bother you?"[7]

NFL AND PRISON PROTESTS

In 2016, Colin Kaepernick, a professional football player, protested racism and police brutality in the United States by kneeling during the national anthem at a football game. He lost his job for beginning this protest, which remains symbolic of race relations. During the 2017 MTV Video Music Awards, Cardi introduced one of the performances. She took the opportunity with cameras on her to announce support for Kaepernick: "As long as you kneel with us, we're going to be standing for you, baby."[8]

Colin Kaepernick, *center*, kneeled during the national anthem at a National Football League (NFL) game to protest racism and police brutality.

In 2018, Cardi B said she wouldn't perform at the Super Bowl until Kaepernick was hired again. She refused a request to perform at the Super Bowl in 2019. Even though she could have made money doing it, and though her husband loves football, she felt she had to support Kaepernick's protest. Even so, Cardi isn't optimistic that there will be significant improvements in the United States soon. She argues that the election of President Donald Trump brought a new surge of racism. "Every artist has

COLIN KAEPERNICK

In 2016, Colin Kaepernick was the first professional football player to kneel during the national anthem in protest. Many people felt he was disrespecting the nation. Kaepernick said, "I am not going to stand up to show pride in a flag for a country that oppresses black people and people of color."[10] He focused especially on acts of police brutality against black people. For almost a year, the NFL banned the protest, but that rule was repealed. No team would hire Kaepernick again after that season. Cardi said she had "mixed feelings" about turning down a Super Bowl performance in 2019, but she knew she had to support Kaepernick for his protest.[11]

explained how harmful he is. He has made divisions in this country," she said in an interview.[9]

In early 2019, Cardi also voiced her concerns about two New York prisons. One inmate was reported dead from a heart attack after a fight with three other inmates. After he died, there was a mix-up over where his body was sent. This led some people, including Cardi and rapper Meek Mill, to suspect a cover-up by law enforcement. Cardi also lent her support to a protest at a federal jail in Brooklyn in February. Because of a power outage, the jail didn't have heat for more than a week. The protest was organized to pressure the jail into ensuring the inmates received proper care. Cardi shared the information about the protest on Instagram.

GOVERNMENT SHUTDOWN

Cardi also spoke up when the US government was partially shut down for more than four weeks in December 2018 and January 2019. Some federal employees were required to work the entire time without pay. After three weeks, President Donald Trump called thousands more employees back to work. Until the government officially resumed, however, nobody would be paid. In a profanity-laced rant, Cardi explained to her more than 40 million followers that it was wrong for people to work without getting paid. Although she said she didn't know how to fix the problem, she was worried for the country.

Commentator Tomi Lahren responded on Twitter to Cardi's political

WHAT IS A SHUTDOWN?

When the US Congress cannot agree about the country's budget, the government can be forced to shut down. Without money, things come to a halt. Some government agencies work at a basic level, and others stop functioning at all. This can go on for as long as it takes for a new budget to be agreed upon. In the case of the 2018–2019 shutdown, a large part of the disagreement was about whether and how much funding should be put toward building a border wall between Mexico and the United States. It was the longest shutdown in national history. When Cardi spoke out against the shutdown, she explained to her followers that the situation negatively impacted everyone, not just people who worked for the federal government.

Cardi B fights back against people who dismiss her opinions because she is a rapper or because of her past as a dancer.

video by sarcastically calling Cardi a "genius political mind."[12] Cardi understood Lahren meant to insult her and threatened to fight Lahren. After several exchanges on Twitter, Cardi said that Lahren was "so blinded with racism" that she could not see how the president was "destroying the country."[13] In the following weeks, Cardi also defended fellow rapper 21 Savage when Lahren tweeted happily about his possible deportation.

The actions of celebrities can shape what is considered normal or good by everyone else. Many celebrities find their decisions spark political discussions they didn't expect. Some people think that entertainers should only entertain. In Cardi's case, people also dismiss her opinions because she used to be a dancer and because of her accent. She has never let other opinions silence her, though. Despite her interest in politics and how vocal she is, Cardi has no plans to run for office. "[I'd] be wrong a lot of times," she said in an interview.[14] But politics aren't only for those in office—voting, debate, and discussion are all excellent ways to participate. For now, Cardi is focusing on those.

"I AIN'T GOT NO TIME TO CHILL"

Despite all her success, Cardi continues to work hard. From awards shows to Netflix shows, recording to touring, she hardly had a day to relax in 2018. As she rapped in "Bodak Yellow," "I ain't got no time to chill."[1] With family, friends, and employees depending on her for work and support, Cardi feels the pressure not to slow down. Throughout the year, though, she had several emotional and exciting new experiences.

In the fall of 2018, auditions began for a new reality show for Netflix. The show, called "Rhythm + Flow," is similar to other music performance competitions. Cardi B, T. I., and Chance the Rapper will be the main judges, joined by representatives of the music industry from each city the show visits. Cardi said she initially agreed to do the show for the money. She is reportedly making $1 million for the first season. During filming, though, she

Cardi B made many appearances during 2019, including at the launch of Kaos Dayclub and Nightclub in Las Vegas, Nevada.

Lady Gaga, *left*, supported Cardi B for her Grammy win.

became attached to some of the contestants. She shared on Instagram how emotional the experience was for her, with only one person able to win the show: "I can't wait for you guys to see this show so y'all can understand how I feel."[2]

Also emotional for Cardi was her chance to meet with
Lady Gaga at the 2019 Grammy Awards. In an interview
about her fashion line, Cardi admitted she likes Lady
Gaga's style. She has been a fan since high school. In
2016, she posted on Instagram that Lady Gaga had been

a major influence on her as a teenager. When a video of a young Cardi performing "Bad Romance" at a high school talent show was put online, Lady Gaga was thrilled. Some insisted Cardi didn't deserve her Grammy, but Lady Gaga spoke up in her defense. The longtime pop star called on fans to "lift [Cardi] up and honor her."[3] Although the two artists admire each other, they had yet to work together as of the 2019 Grammys. Following their meeting at the Grammys, some fans are hoping the two will collaborate.

Frustrated by the negative comments after her Grammy win, Cardi deleted her Instagram account. She restored it just a few days later, though, to announce the release of a new music video. After the video release, "Please Me" jumped to the top of the R&B/Hip-Hop charts for a second week. The song was

DOMINATING THE CHARTS

In March 2019, Cardi B became one of very few artists to replace themselves at the top of the *Billboard* R&B/Hip-Hop chart when her song "Money" was bumped to the Number 2 spot, and "Backin' It Up," by Pardison Fontaine and featuring Cardi, became Number 1. The only other woman to replace herself at the top of the chart was Nicki Minaj in 2015. Minaj has never managed to hold the top three spots at the same time, however. With "Backin' It Up" and "Money" in the top two, and "Twerk" by City Girls featuring Cardi B at Number 3, Cardi is the first woman to hold all three top spots at once.

Cardi's second collaboration with Bruno Mars. In 2018, she was featured on Mars's song "Finesse." The two of them performed together at the Grammys that year.

On the same day that her video for "Please Me" released, Cardi performed at the Houston Livestock Show and Rodeo. While it may seem strange for there to be any music that's not country at a rodeo, it's not new. According to the head of the event, different kinds of music are more likely to bring people to the event who have never been before, as well as a younger audience. Also known as RodeoHouston, the event includes a Black Heritage Day. The head of the event felt that the previous year's Black Heritage Day performance was disappointing for the African American community. He wanted to make up for it. Given Cardi's popularity, it was hoped she would sell more tickets.

Before the rodeo, a petition was signed by more than 18,000 people asking Cardi not to go. The petitioners

CLEAN PERFORMANCES

When most people think of rap, they assume there will be a lot of rude words. Some were concerned that Cardi wouldn't be an appropriate person to perform for the families at RodeoHouston. She has plenty of experience keeping things PG-13, though. She changed some of the words to her songs for her performances on *Saturday Night Live*, at the American Music Awards, and at the Grammys.

"At first people didn't want to play my music on the d*** radio. . . . So I had to keep on making music until I find the right one that's gonna make them catch their eyes on me."[4]
– *Cardi B*

Cardi B's performance at RodeoHouston was one of the best-attended concerts in the rodeo's history.

argued that the rodeo abused animals and Cardi should not support it. Those in charge of the rodeo insisted the animals there were well cared for. They said several veterinarians would be on-site to take care of them if anything should happen. The rodeo also planned to have animal abuse investigators at the event to make sure no animal was mistreated. When the night of her performance arrived, Cardi did perform as planned, and she set a record for attendance at RodeoHouston.

Less than two weeks after the rodeo, Cardi was scheduled to attend the iHeartRadio Music Awards. She was nominated for 14 awards, while the next-most-nominated artist, Drake, was nominated for eight. Cardi took home the award for Best Collaboration for "Finesse" with Bruno Mars. She also became the first woman to win Hip-Hop Artist of the Year. Cardi didn't attend the ceremony to accept her awards. In a video acceptance speech, she said that she was "busy doing a couple things." She thanked her "haters" for motivating her to work harder.[5] As only Cardi would, she also licked the award she was holding in the video.

Cardi performed for the opening weekend of the KAOS club in Las Vegas in April, along with other artists including Alicia Keys and G-Eazy. She had a residency at the club, with several performances there throughout the rest of the year. She also performed at the Coachella Valley Music and Arts Festival that same month. Cardi began 2019 with plans to release her second album during the year. On New Year's Day, she announced she was hoping to put out a record by the spring. Given her many plans for the year, even she said it would be difficult.

RECORD-SETTING PERFORMANCE

Cardi set the new record for attendance at a RodeoHouston performance. Garth Brooks held the record before her, with only three fewer people. Just a few days after Cardi's performance at RodeoHouston, Los Tigres del Norte performed at the rodeo's Go Tejano Day. According to the rodeo, 75,586 people paid to see the group. This beat Cardi's record by six people.[6]

VEGAS RESIDENCY

A residency for an artist means performing regular shows at a single venue, rather than touring. Las Vegas residencies are sometimes thought of as the last stop for an artist on tour. Many artists and groups from the 1990s and 2000s have had residencies there. An increasing number of newer performers are also making agreements for extended stays or repeat performances in the city. Lady Gaga has had a residency there, as well as Pitbull. Some artists use residencies to wind down after whirlwind international tours. Others prefer playing in one location multiple nights in a row.

"If I don't want to work tomorrow, I cannot just stop working, because then, how's other people gonna feed their family? It is a lot of pressure."[8]

— *Cardi B*

Some might expect that artists would relax once they become successful. For Cardi, there is still some anxiety. A lot of people depend on her as their employer, and she wants to help support her family, too. Even in her first few years of fame, she was looking to help her family into better jobs and homes. She was uncomfortable having so much money herself when her parents were working "regula-wage jobs" in the Bronx.[7] In 2018, she finally was able to buy a nice house for her mother.

Cardi didn't rise from working as a dancer in nightclubs to the top of the entertainment business by accident. She has always

Cardi B performed at the Bonnaroo Music and Arts Festival in June 2019.

worked hard, and even with a baby at home she shows no sign of slowing down. She knows the work might not be there tomorrow, so she is careful what she spends today. As the child of immigrants raised in a poor neighborhood and now one of the most famous entertainers in the United States, Cardi B is an example of the American dream. And she's keeping her schedule full so she can keep making those "money moves."[9]

TIMELINE

1992

On October 11, Cardi B is born Belcalis Marlenis Almánzar.

2011

Fired from her job at a grocery store, Cardi begins working as a dancer.

2015

On October 11, Cardi works her last shift as a dancer.

In December, Cardi makes her first appearance on *Love & Hip Hop: New York*.

2016

Cardi's first mixtape, *Gangsta B**** Music, Vol. 1*, is released.

Cardi leaves *Love & Hip Hop* to focus on her music.

2017

On June 16, Cardi's first hit single, "Bodak Yellow," is released.

On September 20, Cardi marries rapper Offset in a secret ceremony.

On October 10, Cardi takes home five awards at the BET Hip Hop Awards ceremony.

2018

In April, Cardi's debut album, *Invasion of Privacy*, is released and immediately tops the charts.

In July, Cardi becomes the first female rapper to have two songs reach Number 1 on the charts.

On July 10, Cardi gives birth to her daughter, Kulture Kiari.

On August 29, a fight breaks out in a club. Cardi is later charged with assault and reckless endangerment.

2018

In September, Cardi throws a shoe at Nicki Minaj during a New York Fashion Week event.

On November 15, Cardi's fashion line with Fashion Nova sells out in less than a day.

2019

In February, Cardi wins the Grammy for Best Rap Album, the first solo woman to do so.

FULL NAME

Belcalis Marlenis Almánzar

DATE OF BIRTH

October 11, 1992

PLACE OF BIRTH

Bronx, New York City

FAMILY

Sister, Hennessy Carolina

EDUCATION

Graduated from Renaissance High School for Musical Theatre and Technology in 2010

CHILDREN

Daughter, Kulture Kiari, born July 10, 2018

CAREER HIGHLIGHTS

Cardi grew her fame through social media and then through reality television until she was able to focus on her music. In 2018, she became the first female rapper to have two of her songs reach Number 1. As of June 2019, she was the only female artist to have five songs in the top ten at the same time. In 2019, she was the first female rapper to win the Grammy Award for Best Rap Album in more than 20 years and the first ever to win it alone.

ALBUMS

*Gangsta B**** Music, Vol. 1* (2016); *Gangsta B**** Music, Vol. 2* (2017); *Invasion of Privacy* (2018)

CONTRIBUTION TO HIP-HOP

Cardi B is an outspoken woman at the top of an industry dominated by men. She is outspoken in favor of political awareness and participation and in defense of women, people of color, and professional dancers.

CONFLICTS

Cardi B's biggest rival is rapper Nicki Minaj, and the two have had an extended feud through social media. In September 2018, Cardi threw a shoe at Minaj and attempted to reach her but was unsuccessful. Cardi once threw a shoe at a castmate during an episode of *Love & Hip Hop: New York*. She was also charged with assault after an incident in a club in New York City.

QUOTE

"Five years ago I was still working hard, just like I'm working today, but I envisioned so little for myself. I settled for so much less."

—*Cardi B*

GLOSSARY

ASTHMA
A medical condition that makes it hard to breathe.

CODE-SWITCHING
Changing one's mannerisms depending on the audience; some people may speak differently at work or school than they do at home.

COLLABORATION
Multiple artists working together on a single track or album.

COMMENTATOR
Someone who comments on and offers his or her opinions on an event or news story.

DEBUT
The first appearance, often of an album or publication, made by a musician or group.

ENTOURAGE
A group of people who support or travel with someone else, usually an important person.

HARASSMENT
Bothering someone, particularly in an aggressive or uncomfortable way.

IMMIGRATE

To come to a country to live.

MISDEMEANOR

A crime with less serious penalties than those assessed for a felony.

MIXTAPE

A compilation of unreleased tracks, freestyle rap music, and DJ mixes of songs.

OBJECTIFY

To present or treat a person like an object.

PRESTIGE

An elevated respect or status.

PUBLICIST

Someone who manages and seeks out opportunities for his or her clients, which may include publicity events.

SINGLE

A song or track released to the public independently, not as part of a complete album.

SELECTED BIBLIOGRAPHY

Estevez, Marjua. "Cardi B Doesn't Give a F***, and Neither Should You." *Vibe*, 15 Nov. 2016, vibe.com. Accessed 15 Apr. 2019.

Grigoriadis, Vanessa. "Cardi B Opens Up about Her 'Rags to Riches' Cinderella Story." *Harper's Bazaar*, 7 Feb. 2019, harpersbazaar.com. Accessed 15 Apr. 2019.

Weaver, Caity. "Cardi B's Money Moves." *GQ*, 9 Apr. 2018, gq.com. Accessed 15 Apr. 2019.

FURTHER READINGS

Bailey, Diane. *Chance the Rapper: Independent Innovator*. Abdo, 2018.

Llanas, Sheila. *The Women of Hip-Hop*. Abdo, 2018.

Oswald, Vanessa. *Hip-Hop: A Cultural and Musical Revolution*. Lucent, 2019.

ONLINE RESOURCES

Booklinks
NONFICTION NETWORK
FREE! ONLINE NONFICTION RESOURCES

To learn more about Cardi B, please visit abdobooklinks.com or scan this QR code. These links are routinely monitored and updated to provide the most current information available.

MORE INFORMATION

For more information on this subject, please contact or visit the following organizations:

BILLBOARD: CHARTS
billboard.com/charts

Billboard magazine, a magazine about the music industry, posts weekly charts showcasing the top music around the world. The Billboard Hot 100 showcases the 100 songs of the week that had the most plays, downloads, and purchases.

NYC: THE OFFICIAL GUIDE
www.nycgo.com

NYC: The Official Guide, created by NYC and Company, helps tourists plan trips to New York City. It provides details on the five boroughs as well as fun things to do and places to stay.

RECORDING ACADEMY
3030 Olympic Blvd.
Santa Monica, California 90404
grammy.com

The Recording Academy is an organization for musicians, songwriters, producers, and others who work in the music industry. It hosts and decides the winners of the Grammy Awards and also runs MusiCares, which provides funding and other support to music artists in need.

SOURCE NOTES

CHAPTER 1. A HISTORIC WIN

1. Keith Caulfield. "Cardi B's 'Invasion of Privacy' Debuts at No. 1 on Billboard 200 Chart." *Billboard*, 15 Apr. 2018, billboard.com. Accessed 19 June 2019.

2. Marjua Estevez. "Cardi B Doesn't Give a F***, and Neither Should You." *Vibe*, 15 Nov. 2016, vibe.com. Accessed 19 June 2019.

CHAPTER 2. COMING UP CARDI

1. Meghan Overdeep. "Cardi B Reveals How She Got Her Unique Name." *InStyle*, 7 Nov. 2017, instyle.com. Accessed 19 June 2019.

2. Andrea Park. "Cardi B Buys Her Mom Her 'Dream Home.'" *W Magazine*, 20 Nov. 2018, wmagazine.com. Accessed 19 June 2019.

3. Angel Diaz. "Too Real: Cardi B Makes Her TV Debut." *Complex*, 15 Dec. 2015, complex.com. Accessed 19 June 2019.

4. Caity Weaver. "Cardi B's Money Moves." *GQ*, 9 Apr. 2018, gq.com. Accessed 19 June 2019.

5. "Cardi B on Her Determination: 'I Get Up Every Single Time, Honey.'" *CBS News*, 9 Dec. 2019, cbsnews.com. Accessed 19 June 2019.

6. Sydney Scott. "Cardi B Says She 'Never Claimed to Be Perfect' after Scamming Video Resurfaces." *Essence*, 26 Mar. 2019, essence.com. Accessed 19 June 2019.

7. Jennifer Drysdale. "Cardi B Responds to Claims She Used to Drug and Rob Men When She Was a Stripper." *ET Online*, 26 Mar. 2019, etonline.com. Accessed 19 June 2019.

8. Anne Victoria Clark. "Cardi B Explains Her Claims that She Drugged and Robbed Men." *Vulture*, 27 Mar. 2019, vulture.com. Accessed 19 June 2019.

9. Diaz, "Too Real: Cardi B Makes Her TV Debut."

10. Marjua Estevez. "Cardi B Doesn't Give a F***, and Neither Should You." *Vibe*, 15 Nov. 2016, vibe.com. Accessed 19 June 2019.

11. Estevez, "Cardi B Doesn't Give a F***."

CHAPTER 3. SOCIAL MEDIA FAME

1. Angel Diaz. "Too Real: Cardi B Makes Her TV Debut." *Complex*, 15 Dec. 2015, complex.com. Accessed 19 June 2019.

2. Rawiya Kameir. "Cardi B's So-Called Life." *Fader*, 29 Feb. 2016, thefader.com. Accessed 19 June 2019.

3. "Cardi B Explains Her Famous Catchphrases." *YouTube*, uploaded by *The Tonight Show Starring Jimmy Fallon*, 10 Apr. 2018, youtube.com. Accessed 19 June 2019.

4. Rawiya Kameir. "Cardi B Did It Her Way." *Fader*, 22 June 2017, thefader.com. Accessed 19 June 2019.

5. Dria Roland. "Cardi B's Success Proves Why She Never Needed 'Love & Hip Hop.'" *Complex*, 12 Apr. 2018, complex.com. Accessed 19 June 2019.

6. Kameir, "Cardi B Did It Her Way."

7. Vanessa Grigoriadis. "Cardi B Opens Up about Her 'Rags to Riches' Cinderella Story." *Harper's Bazaar*, 7 Feb. 2019, harpersbazaar.com. Accessed 19 June 2019.

8. Marjua Estevez. "Cardi B Doesn't Give a F***, and Neither Should You." *Vibe*, 15 Nov. 2016, vibe.com. Accessed 19 June 2019.

9. Beatrice Hazlehurst. "Hennessy Takes Hollywood." *Paper*, 30 Apr. 2018, papermag.com. Accessed 19 June 2019.

10. Kameir, "Cardi B's So-Called Life."

CHAPTER 4. FAMILY AND RELATIONSHIPS

1. Joe Coscarelli. "Emerging from Migos as His Own Man: The Metamorphosis of Offset." *New York Times*, 29 Nov. 2018, nytimes.com. Accessed 19 June 2019.

2. Joanne Kavanagh. "Cardi B Announces She Is Pregnant by Debuting Her Baby Bump on *Saturday Night Live*." *Sun*, 17 May 2018, thesun.co.uk. Accessed 19 June 2019.

3. Mark Savage. "Cardi B Reveals She Married Offset Nine Months Ago." *BBC News*, 26 June 2018, bbc.com. Accessed 19 June 2019.

4. Vanessa Grigoriadis. "Cardi B Opens Up about Her 'Rags to Riches' Cinderella Story." *Harper's Bazaar*, 7 Feb. 2019, harpersbazaar.com. Accessed 19 June 2019.

5. Helen Bushby. "How Do Stars Like Cardi B Juggle Touring with Parenthood?" *BBC News*, 29 July 2018, bbc.com. Accessed 19 June 2019.

6. Savage, "Cardi B Reveals She Married Offset Nine Months Ago."

7. Joelle Goldstein. "Cardi B and Offset Make Their Reunion Red Carpet-Official at the Grammys." *People*, 10 Feb. 2019, people.com. Accessed 19 June 2019.

8. Maria Pasquini. "'Wiser' Cardi B Opens Up about Offset Split." *People*, 9 Dec. 2018, people.com. Accessed 19 June 2019.

9. "Cardi B: 'Money' | 2019 Grammy's Performance." *Grammy Awards*, 2019, grammy.com. Accessed 19 June 2019.

10. Zoe Haylock. "A Complete Timeline of Cardi B and Offset's Complicated Relationship." *Vulture*, 15 Dec. 2018, vulture.com. Accessed 19 June 2019.

CHAPTER 5. PUBLIC REPUTATION

1. Marjua Estevez. "Cardi B Doesn't Give a F***, and Neither Should You." *Vibe*, 15 Nov. 2016, vibe.com. Accessed 19 June 2019.

2. Maria Pasquini. "Cardi B Previously Threw Shoe at *Love and Hip Hop* Star." *People*, 8 Sept. 2018, people.com. Accessed 19 June 2019.

3. "Cardi B: From Stripper to Grammy Award Winner." *BBC News*, 11 Feb. 2019, bbc.com. Accessed 19 June 2019.

4. Jewel Wicker. "Cardi B Defends Publicist after Altercation in Australia." *Fader*, 30 Dec. 2018, thefader.com. Accessed 19 June 2019.

5. Tony M. Centeno. "Cardi B Thinks Her Fight with Nicki Minaj Was Bad for Business." *XXL Mag*, 10 Dec. 2018, xxlmag.com. Accessed 19 June 2019.

6. Dave Quinn. "Mary J. Blige Defends Cardi B amid Grammy Win Backlash." *People*, 15 Feb. 2019, people.com. Accessed 19 June 2019.

7. Joelle Goldstein. "Lady Gaga Defends Cardi B after Some Suggest the Rapper Didn't Deserve Her Win at the Grammys." *People*, 13 Feb. 2019, people.com. Accessed 19 June 2019.

SOURCE NOTES

CHAPTER 6. "TEN DIFFERENT LOOKS AND MY LOOKS ALL KILL"

1. India Pougher and Nerisha Penrose. "Cardi B Wants You to Feel 'Poppin' in Her Fashion Nova Collection." *Elle*, 29 Oct. 2018, elle.com. Accessed 21 June 2019.

2. "Cardi B – Money (Official Audio)." *YouTube*, uploaded by Cardi B, 23 Oct. 2018, youtube.com. Accessed 21 June 2019.

3. "Cardi B & YG – She Bad [Official Audio]." *YouTube*, uploaded by Cardi B, 5 Apr. 2018, youtube.com. Accessed 21 June 2019.

4. Nick Romano. "Cardi B Explains Her Catchphrases to Jimmy Fallon While Co-Hosting the Tonight Show." *Entertainment*, 10 Apr. 2018, ew.com. Accessed 21 June 2019.

5. Brittany Talarico. "Cardi B Wants All the 'Bardashians' to Wear Her Fashion Nova Line—but It's Already Sold Out!" *People*, 15 Nov. 2018, people.com. Accessed 21 June 2019.

6. "ATTENTION, ATTENTION, ATTENTION My FN collection is dropping May 8th. . ." *Instagram*, uploaded by iamcardib, 25 Apr. 2019, instagram.com. Accessed 21 June 2019.

7. Meghan McKenna. "The Cardi B and Azealia Banks Feud, Explained." *Fashion*, 14 May 2018, fashionmagazine.com. Accessed 21 June 2019.

CHAPTER 7. NOT AFRAID TO SPEAK UP

1. Caity Weaver. "Cardi B's Money Moves." *GQ*, 9 Apr. 2018, gq.com. Accessed 19 June 2019.

2. Najma Sharif. "Cardi B Doesn't Need a Degree to Be Feminist, and Non-Black People Don't Get to Politicize Her." *Vibe*, 29 Aug. 2017, vibe.com. Accessed 21 June 2019.

3. Sam Moore. "Cardi B Responds to Claims That Her 'Twerk' Video Undermines the #MeToo Movement." *NME*, 23 Jan. 2019, nme.com. Accessed 21 June 2019.

4. Raquel Reichard. "Woman Crush(ing the Patriarchy) Wednesday: Cardi B." *Latina*, 31 Aug. 2016, latina.com. Accessed 21 June 2019.

5. Shante Honeycutt. "Cardi B Says #MeToo Movement Has Ignored Video Vixens." *Billboard*, 19 Mar. 2018, billboard.com. Accessed 21 June 2019.

6. Jazmine Hughes. "Cardi B on Offset Cheating Rumors and Respecting Strippers." *Cosmopolitan*, 27 Feb. 2018, cosmopolitan.com. Accessed 21 June 2019.

7. Reichard, "Woman Crush(ing the Patriarchy) Wednesday."

8. Brian Josephs. "VMAs 2017: Cardi B Shouts Out Colin Kaepernick." *Spin*, 27 Aug. 2017, spin.com. Accessed 21 June 2019.

9. Madison Feller. "A Comprehensive Guide to the Political Leanings of Cardi B." *Elle*, 26 Feb. 2019, elle.com. Accessed 21 June 2019.

10. Steve Wyche. "Colin Kaepernick Explains Why He Sat during National Anthem." *NFL.com*, 27 Aug. 2016, nfl.com. Accessed 21 June 2019.

11. Jonathan Landrum Jr. "Cardi B Declined Super Bowl Halftime with 'Mixed Feelings.'" *AP News*, 1 Feb. 2019, apnews.com. Accessed 21 June 2019.

12. Emily Heil. "Cardi B Clashes with Conservative Commentator Tomi Lahren over Shutdown." *Washington Post*, 21 Jan. 2019, washingtonpost.com. Accessed 21 June 2019.

13. Heil, "Cardi B Clashes with Conservative Commentator Tomi Lahren over Shutdown."

14. Madison Feller. "Cardi B Knows More about Politics Than You Do." *Elle*, 9 Apr. 2018, elle.com. Accessed 21 June 2019.

CHAPTER 8. "I AIN'T GOT NO TIME TO CHILL"

1. Carl Lamarre. "Here Are Cardi B's 'Bodak Yellow' Title & Lyrics Decoded." *Billboard*, 20 Sept. 2017, billboard.com. Accessed 21 June 2019.

2. Peyton Blakemore. "Cardi B Gets Emotional Talking about Her New Netflix Show." *iHeartRadio*, 30 Jan. 2019, iheart.com. Accessed 21 June 2019.

3. Erica Gonzales. "Lady Gaga Defends Cardi B after She Receives Backlash for Her Grammy Win." *Harper's Bazaar*, 13 Feb. 2019, harpersbazaar.com. Accessed 21 June 2019.

4. Emily Zemler. "Cardi B Takes Over Senior Citizen Center with 'I Like It' on 'Carpool Karaoke.'" *Rolling Stone*, 18 Dec. 2018, rollingstone.com. Accessed 21 June 2019.

5. Liz Calvario. "Cardi B Licks Her Trophy While Accepting Artist of the Year at 2019 iHeartRadio Music Awards." *Entertainment Tonight*, 14 Mar. 2019, etonline.com. Accessed 21 June 2019.

6. Julyssa Lopez. "Los Tigres del Norte Just Broke Cardi B's Houston Rodeo Attendance Record." *Remezcla*, 11 Mar. 2019, remezcla.com. Accessed 21 June 2019.

7. Rawiya Kameir. "Cardi B's So-Called Life." *Fader*, 29 Feb. 2016, thefader.com. Accessed 19 June 2019.

8. Caity Weaver. "Cardi B's Money Moves." *GQ*, 9 Apr. 2018, gq.com. Accessed 19 June 2019.

9. Lamarre, "Here Are Cardi B's 'Bodak Yellow' Title & Lyrics Decoded."

Audrey DeAngelis likes stories and hearing about people and why they do things. That's why she became an anthropologist. She lives in Maryland with her two gerbils, who are not very good researchers but are good at moral support.